Build Your History and Live It Joyfully

Mary Cates Haase

NEW HARBOR PRSS

RAPID CITY, SD

Haase/New Harbor Press
1601 Mt. Rushmore Rd, Ste 3288
Rapid City, SD 5770
www.NewHarborPress.com

Ordering Information:
Quantity sales. Special discounts are available on quantity purchases by corporations, associations, and others. For details, contact the "Special Sales Department" at the address above.

Build Your History and Live It Joyfully / Mary Cates Haase. -- 1st ed.
ISBN 978-1-63357-467-0

Acknowledgements

My heartfelt appreciation to my husband, Phillip Haase, for his encouragement to write this book. His help and unrelenting inspiration enabled me to move forward even when distractions and critics were discouraging. My behind the scenes coach is always my sister, Barb, whose faith in me serves to brighten my life and build my personal history.

To those who read this book, my hope is that you will find encouragement to press forward with your dreams and desires, as you discover that the warmest hug and happiest smile, coupled with truth and goodness, can build your life and your personal history.

Contents

CHAPTER 1

Crush Some Bricks —Tear Down Some Walls —Create Your History

The little nugget of the day might turn out to be the finest part you played all day. Maybe it will be in a handshake, a hug, a smile, a kiss, even a thank-you wave in a traffic jam. Our personal history is perpetually up and running every day. What you and I do to achieve value is up for grabs.

We live in a salad bowl of dynamics every day, characterized by a mix of cultures, rapidly changing technology, and worldwide cyber connectedness. What's more, but sad, we will be *forgotten history* in just two short generations from now. Our life and our personal histories are diminutive, spinning our lives 1,440 minutes every 24 hours. Fortunately, the salad bowl is filled with opportunity and chance happenings, some of which enrich our personal history and maybe enhance someone else's. If the bit part mushrooms, we might accomplish something that carries on from generation to generation, but most likely the history we make is what we do each day in the corner of the world we live in. Whatever yours and my waking moments are, we can bet that a decision and an action of some sort will knock at our door. In a moment of meaningful thought a light bulb in our mind might get switched on, or a sudden brain wave might spark enthusiasm to try something wild and out of the ordinary. Whatever we do, whatever we leave undone or allow to keep incubating in our minds, the time is now to act and put another benchmark on life.

We humans are basically beginnings and endings. The in-between is what counts. The phone calls, email letters, text messages, meetings, and conversations with colleagues and family members are what move us every day. Hopefully, you believe that most anything is possible at any age as long as it's sane. Even the daily twists and turns bursting with hard bumps and deep potholes has good reason to keep us enthusiastic. There are millions of possibilities waiting for the entrepreneurs of life! Even in a wheelchair, we can find people full of grit who know that the way to survive is to never give up. Passion for goals and self-worth is bully-smart living for everyone. Wise people courageously move forward. They keep crunching financial figures, patiently wait for healing, forgiving themselves for failure, and most of all they resist temptation to cave in. They keep crushing the bricks that get in the way, tearing down the walls, and creating a meaningful personal history.

There will never be another John the Baptist, of whom Jesus said was the greatest born of a woman. There will never be another woman like Mary to give birth to a baby without the sperm of a man. There's only been one mighty apostle Paul, who preached to thousands of lost souls in Asia, and started the first Christian churches. Still, we are great in whatever God has done in our lives, and the good thing is that He isn't finished with us yet. You are still breathing and reading this book.

Paul was a history maker. While traveling to Rome as a prisoner, because he was angrily arrested for preaching the gospel of Jesus Christ, he was shipwrecked on an island. As the boat tossed and twisted on the violent waves prior to crashing on offshore rocks, he knew that he and the other prisoners would end up having to swim to safety. Pushing all fear aside, he let his faith that God would save them go to work. In foresight, he understood that they would need physical strength to swim to safety once the boat crashed. Picture him trying to steady his feet and remain standing as he yelled orders to the other prisoners above the sound of roaring waves. "We have to eat for strength if we're going to swim and survive!"

Miraculously, no one lost their life. They remained stranded on the island until taken to a Roman prison. During the time he spent on the island he was bitten by a poisonous snake, but survived. Undoubtedly saved again due to God's plan for his life. He healed many of the sick there and turned hearts to believe in Jesus Christ. Never stopping to question God's plan or mourn over the painful wounds healing from the frantic swim to shore among jagged rocks. The letters he later wrote to his new churches became the bulk of the New Testament we read today.

Your history and mine will seldom go past our immediate family, workplace, close friendships, or club memberships and church. But thinking beyond that, we have great influence in our casual hellos and our occasional handshakes, even impromptu conversations with strangers. A once-in-a-lifetime opportunity might pop up unexpectedly, and suddenly we know we are right where we're meant to be. Though we live circumspectly each day, the nuggets are waiting. And sometimes unaware, the bit part we played toppled a wall by what we said, or helped in a moment of helplessness, maybe saved someone's soul from the junk pile. Unaware, we might create an oasis of grace in the hug we gave impromptu or that smile we flashed, or the meaty handshake we offer. The bit parts most often are the best nuggets of the day.

The people we pass by are not wearing T-shirts that say *"I need to be loved"* or *"I'm terminally ill and need support."* That little kid hanging onto his mother's skirt at the bus stop is not crying because he got spanked, but because he's hungry. The person sitting in the pew in front of us at church is not waving a flag and chanting that they are lonely, but inside they are slowly dying. It's often without a tear or a waving flag that we encounter someone who needs our smile and a physical touch. A hug may tell them they are truly worthy to be alive. To simply stop for a moment and look into the immense diversity of human dynamics surrounding us, there are plenty of opportunities to take our personal history up a notch each day. The salad bowl is filled with all sorts of ideas and opportunities.

I've never meant a person with the sharply intelligent brain that Albert Einstein had, but I agree with his vital opinion about life and happiness. He is quoted, saying, "If you want to live a happy life, tie it to a goal, not to people or things." That might sound selfish, but without a goal there generally are no friendships or inspirations to get out of bed each morning. His words become more appealing when he said, "Imagination is more important than knowledge, because knowledge is limited, whereas, imagination encircles the world." An Einstein moment for us might be to simply act upon an idea that could end in a happy result, or do something daring, but rational. Treading on the edge says life is still in you, and the brink is where you should be for the moment. It is not just the schizophrenics in the world who hear voices. On a sane note, it is the person who knows that his or her history is important, and what they accomplish might help their, or someone else's, day get better. Who knows, you might save someone who is living like they can't get to hell fast enough. Think of yourself as a sounding board of insights, prompters, or homilies that look deep, not just on the surface. Every day, the clock is marking off your *moments in time* and you are creating your personal history.

We are not little islands, peppered across the map of the world. We are people that other people see and often take note of. As John Donne wrote: "No man is an island entirely of itself, —every man is a piece of the continent, a part of the main." *We are the world,* so to speak. We are part of the core, the key and the foremost. Our *once in history* is spinning our lives each day. Every life has history-making opportunities. Never be a rebel against yourself. Take the history-making moments as though someone is handing you a billion-dollar bank check. Opportunities come and go like the weather, and visitors and relationships do the same. Don't miss the times to crush some bricks, tear down some walls, and build an oasis of profitable history.

Discussion

Read Philippians 4:13 and answer the question: Is this promise of accomplishing all things through Christ appropriate for my goals; and, if so, how can I begin moving forward?

Does fear of failure hold you back from accomplishing your desires and goals? Read Isaiah 41:10 and write the promises that are in this scripture.

What are the things you desire to accomplish and how can you move them into history-making accomplishments? Read 2 Corinthians 12:9 and discuss the promise of Christ's power in your life.

CHAPTER 2

Something Sacred Happens at the Dinner Table

Company was coming for dinner and I was in search of the meatiest ham in the store's meat cooler to serve to my guests. My shopping cart already held the sliced pineapple and maraschino cherries that would dress the ham to the nines. I pushed and shoved the hams around in the cooler as though I were hunting for a golden treasure. That was exactly what I wanted—the best and most impressive ham ever. When I found it, and placed it into the cart, I was shocked to see that the fake acrylic nail on the index finger of my right hand was missing. Heavens to Murgatroyd! My aggressive ham-pushing obviously put too much pressure on the nail, even though scientific UV rays had changed it into some sort of cement, which would last for at least two weeks. I panicked! Any perfectionist would panic, knowing how weird their hand would look while sitting at an elegant dinner table, missing a beautifully shaped red fingernail. Panting, because I was out of breath from tossing and rolling around every ham in the cooler, I quickly envisioned myself sitting at the head of the table, lifting my water glass to my lips with everyone's eyes seeing a missing nail. Then I thought, if I could find the nail, I might be able to super glue it back on.

It didn't matter that the meat cooler was deep and cold and my hands were already cold with a shade of blue. The numbness was trivial. I had to find that nail. I dived back into the cooler, frantically searching, but it was useless. I was no better off than someone searching for a small bolt in a scrapyard filled with thousands of banged-up cars and rusted sheet metal. Then, the thought came that I may have lost the nail in the produce department while rummaging through unshucked ears of corn. At the corn bin, I was in that same anxious spirit, searching for the most beautiful, most luscious ears. Nothing wrong with wanting the best, but it wasn't the ham and the corn that was full of pride, it was me. I whipped my cart around and rolled it over to the corn bin. No one needed to know I was searching for a fingernail, not if I made it look legit that I needed more corn. That search was useless, too. The fake nail was lost somewhere in that store, and most likely would be a shudder of ick to whomever discovered it.

Somehow, the dinner turned out okay because no one was examining my hands. Before they arrived, I managed to find a bottle of red fingernail polish and did my best to make the finger look like it fit in with the rest, although the nail was much shorter. My guests enjoyed themselves, and the conversations were good. The best part of the dinner was the fellowship we shared with warm camaraderie around the table. Secretly, my pride was being marched to the guillotine, as I realized what mattered was the *sacred something* that happened at that table.

Perfectionist dinners with friends have commonly turned into delivered lukewarm pizza, a bag of precut salad, and a good movie. Pizza and movies are the norm in our world of extreme casualness. Sadly, the *holy thing* that happens at the supper table has been lost. More often we meet in restaurants. It saves us from cooking and cleaning. However, I have to say that on the opposite side, some of the best visits I've enjoyed in my *personal history* are those not spent in a perfect Martha Stewart house, but one with a little bit of messiness and a few dirty dishes in the kitchen sink. That atmosphere says to me that I can fully relax and not have to be a perfect guest. Go—go ahead, unwind and genuinely enjoy "chilling out."

Growing up in Detroit, my parents rented out a little house that was built on our property behind our family house. Most neighbors had their garages there. Instead, we had a four-room house with one bathroom. An old lady I called Aunt Laura, and her middle-aged single son, Oliver, rented that little house. My mom and Aunt Laura shared the backyard and the clothesline on certain days of the week. There were times when Oliver was not at home, so Aunt Laura would knock on our back door and visit with us. One day, she came to our door while my mom was cooking spaghetti for supper. Now, you need to know that my mom's spaghetti was far from Italian cuisine, however, the delicious aroma filled our house and created anxious appetites.

The recipe was simple. A mixture of browned hamburger and chopped onions, soft-boiled spaghetti pasta, and Campbell's tomato soup. I loved it. So, on with the story of Aunt Laura coming to our door late that afternoon and sitting down at our kitchen table. She talked to my mom while the aroma of fried hamburger and chopped onions filled our small kitchen. I loved to sit and listen to this old lady. She was a tiny woman whose head and hands shook very badly. She had developed what medical science calls an *essential tremor* that was common and nothing to worry about. I never saw someone so notoriously skilled at handling a cup of coffee while shaking like a leaf in a thunderstorm, and not spill any of it. That day, when Mom was ready to call us to the table, she asked Aunt Laura if she would like to stay and have supper with us. I can still hear her happy voice when she said, "Oh, yes," and added, "I do love baghetti." I put my hands over my mouth and choked back laughing, because I saw my mother's stern face looking at me, silently saying, don't you dare laugh at how she pronounces spaghetti. Believe me, you had to be there, seeing this old lady's head bobbing back and forth and hearing the word *"baghetti"* coming from her lips. For years later, my brother and I would laugh and call our spaghetti dinners, *baghetti dinners*. But it wasn't just the word that gave us fun and laughter, it was the closeness we had with this precious old woman. We felt the holy thing that happens around the table when you eat and break bread together. I came to love Aunt Laura dearly.

Other renters came and went, and there were other times when coffee and cookies were shared with them, even a fun table game like Chinese checkers. (Oh yes, Aunt Laura played Chinese checkers with us, and often the marbles rolled all over the board when it was her turn. I dared not laugh then, either.) There were occasions when, around the kitchen table, renters would tell of their troubles, and my godly parents would do what they could to help solve their problems. The table seemed to be a sacred place. Not exactly like my dad's pulpit at our church, where he fed the gospel message to the attenders, but a place where people sat and experienced a little bit of help and heaven.

Indeed, dear old Aunt Laura and others were graciously taken into my parents' loving care during their lonely and needy hours, which brings up the point that many people today are not as fortunate as these renters were, having people in their lives like my parents. Today, many hungry souls slip by unnoticed and unwanted in a busy world that tops more than eight billion people. It might shock us to know how many people in the United States are hungry for something other than food. Something more than a kitchen table and a shared cup of coffee, but rather someone genuinely interested in them, but that's another chapter in this book.

It was not just Aunt Laura who made history in my life during the years I was a kid growing up in a crowded Detroit neighborhood, but two other neighbors who lived in the house next door. Strange that they never knew us. They were the Italians, fresh from the shores of Italy, struggling with the English language. The hermits of the neighborhood. I don't remember my parents having much to do with them because they chose to be recluse. But what made history about them in my life was their garden and the wonderful smell of simmering tomatoes that came through their screened kitchen door.

Their garden reached from their back porch all the way to the alley behind the neighborhood, and luscious tomatoes covered their plot of earth. They staked the heavy plants using scraps of torn cloth and picked ripened tomatoes all summer long. The most wonderful smells of bubbling stewed tomatoes, most likely thickening into a thick tomato garlic-basil sauce, wafted their way into our backyard and sometimes through our screened kitchen door. I would have helped pick and peel tomatoes for the chance to sit at their table and eat. They never knew how much I loved the wonderful smells that came from their kitchen. I should have told them, because they created a bit part in my personal history.

The 1967 movie *Guess Who's Coming to Dinner* explored the complexities of racism and prejudice through the lens of an interracial couple. Odd, it wasn't the bedroom that was the take-off at the beginning of this love story. It was the dining room table. In 1967, most families were eating together. Elegant dinner parties were common, and Sunday dinner with family and roast chicken with dressing was special. Today it's another story. Google the question *How many families sit down and eat together?* and be shocked that the answer is less than half. Lots of reasons for this, and the main problem is that parents and kids have little time left because of work schedules and after-school activities. The Old Testament prophet Daniel penned words of prophecy from God describing a major change from the world back then, with a slow-paced sandal foot and camel travel, to great knowledge and fast travel from one end of the earth to the other. (Daniel 12:4) We have the fulfillment of this prophecy, and with it are all sorts of changes, including the obvious that even the dinner table would become a TV tray in front of a glassy screen of color and movement.

But now, to finish the story of old Aunt Laura. She died in that little house when I was twelve years old. She simply got up from her chair one evening and dropped to the floor. She was gone by the time Oliver laid her on the bed. Immediately she became "past history," and much of my early childhood history that was shared with her, centered around a small kitchen table while she talked to my mother, ate baghetti, played Chinese checkers, and made me giggle behind her back. I felt much sorrow that she was gone, and decades later, I am still thinking of her and writing about her.

Wonderful things can happen at the dinner table. I like to call it the "supper table," because *supper* has a nostalgic ring to it. Sometimes I think, just for a moment, I would like to step into the past and be a child again and see the streetlight come on and know it was time for me to go home to supper. Like the lyrics of the song "Come Home It's Suppertime," singing the words that went something like this: *I used to play until evening shadows came, then walking home I could hear my mother call my name, come home it's suppertime.*

Searching through past history-making events in my life, decades back in Detroit, I think of the house I grew up in, the simple food we ate, the play, the joy, and the hurt. Though I am a happy person, mysteriously, I spend long moments wishing to spend just one day back, sitting at our kitchen table, even wanting to sniff the sweet metallic odor of diesel fuel coming from old trucks and buses. Such nonsense, but maybe not. For in remembering the past, anything new that comes to us often comes at the expense of something in our past—like the death of someone you have loved.

Friend, never miss an opportunity to enjoy sacred time spent seated at the table with family and friends.

Discussion

Think about past suppers/dinners with your family and compare them to your gatherings today. Would you say they were more intimate and meaningful back then, and, if so, how and why?

Read Matthew 9:10-17. Why do you believe Jesus ate with sinners? Does He set a good example today of hospitality?

A direct command to Christians is given in 1 Peter 4:9, that we entertain without complaint or reluctance. If we see it as a task, how might we see it more as a privilege and honor? Hebrews 13:2 says we might have shown hospitality to angels without knowing.

CHAPTER 3

Only the Lonely

The long coach ride that stopped in Bradford, Iowa, in 1857 spawned a song from Dr. William S. Pitts, titled "The Church in the Wildwood." The lyrics tell of a sweet Sabbath morning where a church bell rings in the dell, and the hollow is full of trees and beautiful wildflowers. No spot is so dear to his childhood than the little brown church in the wildwood. This little church is gone, and all that it held sacred is gone, including warm welcomes and hefty handshakes, perhaps an invitation to Sunday potluck dinner. Here in the twenty-first century, thousands of churches are sprinkled like pepper across the globe, but similar to the little brown church in the wildwood, much of what they used to be is gone. The lonely person who is seeking friendship comes to church and too often finds no help there. It's like attending a theater or movie. You walk in and listen and leave without any words spoken to you. The only difference is that you paid to watch the show.

Loneliness has a way of growing, like peat moss edging its way in the shadows of Kentucky Blue grass, to take it over. The lyrics of the song "Only the Lonely," written by Roy Orbison, say it well. The song says only the lonely know how it feels to be lonely. They know the feeling isn't right, and they cry. Like a ship sailing in the dark of night with no land in sight, the feeling of loneliness can seem like cold shivers and the need for a warm blanket and a hot cup of chocolate. Hundreds of situations, coupled with the right state of mind, can bring on the feeling that we are alone in the world and no one really loves us or cares.

The lonely are everywhere. They are in shopping malls, airports, hair salons and barber shops, in line at the grocery store, and most often sitting in the waiting room among the other lonely at the psychologist's office. The lonely may smile, might laugh when appropriate and give a snug hug or a meaty handshake and we'll never guess that inside the empty spaces of their hearts they are slowly dying. You might be one of those lonely people in the world, and if so, it is a sad and serious matter.

Oddly enough, the famous are often lonely. Abraham Lincoln was lonely and much hated. Some thought he was responsible for the deaths of those who died during the Civil War. In his lonely state, he was assassinated. Winston Churchill was lonely and fought the black dog of depression with only a few knowing. Michael Phelps, the Olympic swimmer, has stated that he struggles with loneliness, including a period after the 2012 Games when he felt suicidal. As his battle with depression continued, he sought professional help and was hospitalized. He has spoken publicly many times of his struggle. Loneliness is no respecter of persons. The rich and famous, even children, are subject to its ruin.

A true story of loneliness unfolded many decades ago in the fourth-grade classroom at the Hutchinson Elementary School in Detroit. History was made that day in the lives of fifteen kids. I'm one of them! It was soon to be Valentine's Day, and to our delight, the teacher said we could exchange Valentine's cards and have cupcakes on that special day. My mother bought a large package of Valentine's cards for me, and I had the pleasure of signing the cards and addressing the envelopes. The schoolroom party was full of fun while we exchanged Valentine's cards and ate cupcakes. On the way home, joy was bubbling up in my heart, and I couldn't wait to show my mother the cards I received. But the next day, the joy ended when the teacher scolded us because one of the students did not receive a card. It was a girl who sat very quietly every day, and none of us noticed her much. We forgot her. I remember feeling ashamed, but also lucky it wasn't me who was left out. The teacher told us to bring a Valentine's card to her the next day. I didn't have any cards left, so I erased a signature on a card someone gave to me and put my name on it.

I remember getting up out of my chair and giving this for-gotten girl my card the next day. It probably said what cards say today: *"You're sweeter than strawberries," "You're so nice. Be my Valentine,"* and *"You're like candy, I like you."* Most likely, the eraser made some smudges on the card I gave her, and today, as I re-member this event, it makes me feel sad all over again. I'm sure the smudges made her feel the hurt worse. After all, who would get excited about a secondhand Valentine's card? For all of us kids, our turn was coming, because no one's history is void of loneliness. Even with a circle of family and friends around us, that little black dog nips and barks.

Loneliness might be considered a learned emotion or labeled as a temptation to indulge in for some psychological reason. The story of a poor traveling peddler who sells rattraps seriously considers this thought. The peddler begins to see the world as a rattrap that lures people in with luxury and materialistic pleasures, thus, trapping themselves by their own desires. This well-known saga refers to a person experiencing deep loneliness in the book titled *The Rattrap* by Selma Lagerlof, and it brings this thought up for consideration. The peddler meets a farmer who lives in a small cottage and offers him shelter and warmth for a moment of human connection and compassion. As they talk, the peddler begins to question the crofter's outlook on life. The crofter most likely understands the peddler's suspicious view of mankind as a false conception and wants to straighten out his warped mindset. He believes the man should be experiencing a flicker of conscience, at least. But sadly, he is unable to help him escape his solitary existence. The peddler's inward loneliness traps and ensnares him. Could it be that he loves the loneliness he lives in? Indeed, it might be a learned behavior.

For people like the rattrap peddler, if love and friendship are to come, it will require taking some risks and owning some responsibility. But strangely, for many, it becomes easier to walk alone. Like the lyrics of the song, "I'll Walk Alone," it implies the truth that it's easier for some to be lonely because love is lost.

You may remember the film, "Over the Hedge." The animals require few means to achieve their goals. They simply eat and hibernate and amuse themselves watching the complex lives of the film's human characters. (That would be us!) To them, it seems that we humans live the most hectic and lonely lifetimes. Maybe that's right for the great majority of us. It's not uncommon for goal-conscious people to operate in frenzied lives and be threatened with loneliness. The difference comes in knowing that your life and your history has purposeful meaning. So, here comes the appropriate sermon . . . Knowing Jesus and living in His principles and precepts brings purpose to life, and peace with the assurance of eternal life. He said, "I chose you, and I give you work to do that is purposeful, so that you can accomplish things that will last." (Paraphrased, John 15:16) End of sermon. The doxology: If you are lonely, Jesus will be your best friend.

The black dog comes and nips in different ways, even when surrounded by admirers and an audience offering you a standing ovation. There's no offseason. Things come and go, and the twists are numerous. Many of those who reach high levels of achievement know its mysterious darkness. Maybe this is you, struggling in the pit, and the only way out is that you must trust God to pull you out. Or maybe, life is great right now and you need no one, but God may have a lonely person waiting for your smile and a happy bear hug. We might be the person to walk the lonely road with a widow struggling with depressive isolation. We might be the person who leads a little frightened child to Jesus. Maybe it's a stretch of the imagination, but you or I might be the person that saves a certain *George Bailey* from jumping off the bridge on Christmas Eve.

The end of the story is yours. Once upon a time there lived *you*, and you lived happily ever after, making lonely people feel worthy and loved. Your personal history is yours.

Discussion

How many ways can you put John 15:16 to work in your life? Do you attend a church that greets visitors with warm welcomes and follows up with them? If your church does not warmly welcome visitors, how could you help in that area of neglect?

Jot down the name of someone you suspect is lonely and make a point to contact them. Maybe invite them to lunch and include an invitation to come to church if they do not attend.

CHAPTER 4

Welcome the Day God Shows You Your Junkyard

It's been called the *Jesus moment*, the recognition that life has become cluttered with ruin and help from God is needed. This epiphany is something that might be viewed as a metaphor, meaning that the junkyard dweller gets on his knees and acknowledges before God that they are sinners and the muddle they are living in needs major help. When the truth of ruin comes to light, the messed-up life can be identified as a junkyard of devastating wreckage. Owning up to the truth is personal, but it is vital to acknowledge if God is going to lead the person out of the junkyard mess. Welcome the day God exposes your junkyard.

The conversion of Saul (later named Paul) in Acts chapter 9 of the Bible is an excellent example of a Jesus moment. Saul was heavy into a campaign against anyone who believed in Jesus Christ. He had a letter from the high priest giving consent to persecute Christians, and thus advance his career and build up his reputation as a true Pharisee. No matter if they were men or women, if he knew they were believers in Jesus, he would take them prisoner and deliver them to Jerusalem.

Paraphrasing the biblical story, Saul passively stood by and watched a furious crowd in the act of fatally stoning a believer in Christ named Steven. He heard the man cry out, "Lord Jesus, receive my spirit." He saw the man kneel and pray, "Lord, do not hold this sin against them." In earnest resolve to jail all believers in Jesus, Saul's rampage required him to journey on to Damascus. This road was the perfect place for God to show Saul the junkyard of skepticism and cruelty in which he was operating. Suddenly, a bright light from heaven flashed around him and around the men who were journeying with him. So bright and piercing was the light that he fell to the ground and heard a voice saying, "Saul, Saul, why do you persecute me?" His answer back is indicative that he sensed a strong, piercing authority speaking to him. He responded by saying, "Who are you, Lord?" The Lord answers, "I am Jesus whom you are persecuting by terrorizing my believers. Get up and go into the city, and you will be told what you must do." The men traveling with him stood shaking and speechless. They saw no one, just a flash of bright light coming out of the sky, and heard a shocking voice. Saul pulled himself up and opened his eyes to find that he was blind. Taking him by the hand, the men led him to Damascus. There, he stayed in the house of a man named Judas (not the Judas who betrayed Jesus). He remained blind and did not eat or drink for three days.

Imagine the physical shock this dramatic scene portrays—a mysterious encounter with Jesus that exposes the terroristic junkyard Saul was operating in. By shocking him with a split-second flash of light so bright that it blinds him, Saul is faced with the consequences of his heartless campaign. He cowers and answers the voice commanding him to follow instructions. This staggering encounter might run second to the 2012 movie *Sinister*, which was cited as the scariest movie of all time, based on heart rate data of those watching it in the theater. It championed a scare score of 96.

At the same time of this event in Damascus there lived a man by the name of Ananias, whom the Lord spoke to in a vision, telling him to go to the house of Judas and ask for a man from Tarsus named Saul. At this same time, Saul was frightfully praying and he too had a vision of a man named Ananias who would come to him and place his hands on him to restore his sight. God was working his glorious plan, which was to anoint Saul to bring the truth of Jesus Christ to the Gentiles and become the greatest ambassador for Jesus the world would ever know. Who would have ever thought that Saul of Tarsus would become an ambassador for Jesus Christ! For that matter, who would believe that you or I might be the one person God wants to deliver a message of Christ Jesus to someone who is lost in a self-made junkyard? Or could you be recognizing the same bright light that Saul was blinded by?

Ananias was frightened because he had heard about Saul and how ruthless he was. His conversation with God disclosed his fear, as he reasoned that he knew Saul was on his way to

Damascus with a letter from the high priest, which would give him authority to jail any believer in Jesus. The Lord convinces him by explaining to him who this Jesus persecutor is going to become—the world's greatest evangelist, and his name is going to be changed to Paul. The conversation between Ananias and Jesus might have gone something like this: "Man up, Ananias! Go to this man named Saul, for he is my chosen instrument to carry on my name before the Gentiles, and to their kings and before the people of Israel. I am going to show him how he will suffer for my name. So, pull yourself together because I'm commanding you to give this man my message, and to anoint him for the work he is going to do."

It's not unusual for a person to experience an unexpected moment of Holy Spirit contact and a realization that something of awesome power is giving instructions—strong enough to move the person to obey the command. Obviously, Ananias was convinced of the power speaking to him, and he did as he was directed and entered the house where Saul was staying in. Boldly, he placed his hands on him and said, "Brother Saul, the Lord Jesus who spoke to you on your way to Damascus has sent me to touch you so that your sight will return, and that the power of the Holy Spirit will fill you." Immediately, Saul's sight was returned to him, and he was baptized. From that time on, the life story of Saul moved on dramatically, as his name was changed to Paul and he followed the Lord as his chosen instrument. He preached and taught the good news of Jesus Christ throughout Asia Minor. Churches were established, and his letters to them became the bulk of the New Testament. Truly, a miraculous conversion from a life in the junkyard of abusive persecution against believers in Jesus, to gaining more and more converts for the kingdom of God. Indeed, welcome the day God exposes your junkyard.

Fast forwarding to another note of miraculous conversions, the famous British author and philosopher C.S. Lewis was an atheist for many years. Although there were no bright lights radiating from heaven to turn him to the Lord, Lewis reached a wonderful conversion. It's worth telling!

He was born in Belfast, Ireland, and was experiencing a happy childhood until, at nine years old, his mother died. His father was unable to manage his grief and, at the same time, take care of C.S. and his brother—consequently, he shipped them off to a boarding school. After college, Lewis joined the fight in World War I. The severity and cruelty of the war angered him severely, making him doubt that God ever existed. His incense led him away from the church.

While at Oxford, he joined a group that met each week to read and discuss each other's literary work. One of the fiercest atheists that Lewis knew in this group admitted that the Gospel was good, and it appeared to him that God had entered into human history. His admission about God brought curiosity to dance in Lewis's mind. He began to look at things seriously. The crux of his atheism began to crumble, and in hindsight shows evidence that God was at work to transform his life, much like the life of Saul. We might stop for a moment at this point to consider that every conversion is solid evidence that God is at work in all of us.

Voicing multiple questions and showing an agreed lenience toward the existence of God and His plan of salvation brought some of Lewis's friends to gang up on him. I guess it was as though they were saying to him, how dare you even hint to believe in God, much less believe as Lewis's own spoken words say: *That which I greatly feared had at last come upon me. I finally gave in and admitted that God was God, and knelt and prayed: perhaps, that night [I was] the most dejected and reluctant convert in all England." Saying this, however, did not wholly convert me to Christianity. That came two years later while traveling to a zoo in a sidecar. When we set out, I did not believe that Jesus Christ was the Son of God, but when we reached the zoo, I did. I had not exactly spent the journey in thought nor in great emotion. 'Emotion' is perhaps the last word we can apply to some of the most important events. It was more like a man, after a long sleep . . . and becomes aware that he is now awake. From death to life. From darkness to light. The fog had lifted, and the Son was now shining bright.* (Quote from the book *Surprised by Joy*, by C.S. Lewis)

So, it seems that C.S. Lewis woke up from the junkyard of intellectual disbelief to truly believe that God is who He says He is. His writings and lectures testify that he had a warlike struggle that eventually led to Jesus Christ and showcased worldwide his creative talent and the gifts God bestowed on him.

History goes on in the realm of junkyard conversions. Many do not know that Franklin Graham, the son of evangelist Billy Graham, didn't want God running his life. He was quoted as saying, "I wanted to have fun. I went to church because I was expected to. As I got older in my teenage years, I was more interested in pleasing myself. I just turned my back on God and tried to serve myself."

He reflects upon his conversion by saying that the more he sought to please himself, the more he became unhappy. "One night, I just got on my knees, and I said, 'God, I've sinned against you and I'm sorry.'" As he allowed God to take the pieces of his life and use them, he became one of the best-known Christian evangelists and the founder of Samaritan's Purse.

The human junkyard can be many things, —from disbelief and defiance against God to selfishness, unrighteous anger, and so on. I like to think of God as the hound dog of heaven, seeking those who are lost. Once He corners the person and the truth becomes transparent and unmistakable, the look back becomes a welcome sign that God showed them the junkyard of their life.

Discussion

Read Romans 1:20–21 and contemplate the visible attributes of God's power and His "visual existence." List the known things that make it impossible for people to claim ignorance.

After believing in Jesus Christ and accepting Him as your Savior, have you had doubts about your salvation? Read the assurance of salvation in Romans 8:1-4. Think about the love of God in Christ Jesus to forgive and never take back your salvation.

In Satan's vast arsenal of tricks to keep a person in the junkyard of sin and disbelief, be assured that all true believers in Christ Jesus are safe in Him, regardless of how the enemy tries to discourage them. Satan is the accuser. Read Revelation 12:10.

CHAPTER 5

Morning Cobwebs

In the wee hours of the morning, the light of the streetlamp shines through the blinds, making patterns of soft dancing shadows on the adjacent wall. Far across the sea, half the world is wide awake, and so are you. Sleep is not knocking and your thoughts jump from one subject to another. Your mind feels like it is filled with cobwebs. You're tired, but you can't drift off to sleep. Tomorrow you will be in contact with many people while you burrow your way through several errands. Your personal history will start when you leave the house —perhaps before you leave. For sure, when you grab your coat and you're out the door, something you say or do might live forever.

Finally, morning comes, and at breakfast you read the devotion for the day from your inspirational booklet and pray the ritual prayer. There's no excitement in your request for God to graciously direct your day and keep you safe. Today, it seems just repetition. Will the cobwebs clear?

A *cobweb* is essentially an abandoned spiderweb that has collected dust after the spider moved on. It can trap other particles in the air, making it more pronounced. Nothing living enters an abandoned web, and today, your brain feels like a vacant jungle. Your teenage daughter grabs her backpack and kisses you goodbye. An old Chinese proverb whizzes its way into your mind. *Passionate kiss like the spider's web soon leads to undoing the fly.* Maybe the cobweb will fade away and today will be a great personal history-making day.

Nearing the first stop on your list of things to do, you find cars parked bumper-to-bumper at the curb of the business office you need to enter. Annoyed, you turn the corner and drive to the back-alley area and park. Inside the building you find everyone busy at their desk. It's up to you to get noticed. Someone looks up and says hello. Your day's history is starting to be played out, but nothing unusual happens here. Your business gets finished and the next stop is the bank.

At the bank, you encounter three busy tellers manning their windows. Five people are in line in front of you while you wait. Business moves slow, and your turn finally comes with a pretty teller who greets you warmly and asks how your day is going. Bingo! A gem of an opportunity to experience something good in your day and add to your personal history. It's an easy chance to turn the conversation back to her instead of telling her how your day is going. Maybe she needs a compliment along with your smile. The cobweb starts to clear. You tell her your day is fine and ask how her day is going. She responds and says it's a busy day, with a tone that hints that she is experiencing overload. This is your golden opportunity to bring the conversation around to her. You ask her what she's going to do when she leaves at the end of her day. She looks at you as though a ray of sunshine suddenly weaved its way through her frenzied morning. She tells you that she'll pick up her toddler from day care. Her smile says it all. You have reminded her of the one special gift in her life that is the reason she is working. Keep grabbing the moment! It's fully yours now. "What's her name?" you ask. "Olivia," she says with a big smile. You can see that she's brushing off her monotonous day of money changing and cashing checks, while she counts the cash you requested. "How old is she?" you ask. The teller slips your cash into an envelope and tells you that her little one is three years old. As you take the envelope, you say, "I'll bet she's always waiting for you to pick her up each day." The teller chuckles and says, "Yes, and she jabbers all the way home." While you tuck the envelope into your purse, you say, "God bless you and your little one." She smiles while you turn and head toward the door, giving you a little jab in your heart that you know those few moments with her were good because you brightened her day by simply asking the right questions. Now you drive to the next stop—the grocery store—to pick up milk and lettuce. This is the last stop. You're hungry and in a hurry to get home because you skipped most of your breakfast. Chick-fil-A is on the way home and chicken strips and waffle fries sound great.

Just inches from you in the produce department, a middle-aged woman is probing for a head of lettuce. You stand there waiting your turn and sense that she sees you in the corner of her eye, but she doesn't step to the side to let you in. Unless you get aggressive and reach to grab a head, you're going to wait at her command. It's obvious she's hogging the bin, maybe deliberately. People are mean today, which makes you think that Satan is busy orchestrating his prize people against Christians. The small revolver in your purse also reminds you that the world is extremely evil and you will take no forceful action upon anything that can be avoided—which means no emotional Kamikaze driving when someone cuts you off and gives you the middle finger, and no pushing your way into the lettuce bin. You continue to wait, and there's no cobweb operating here. You consider striking up a conversation. You could say something like, "How funny it is that when searching for the best head of lettuce, they suddenly all start looking the same." The moment is yours. How much creative nerve do you have? Finally, the woman plops a head of lettuce in her cart and leaves.

The lettuce and milk are bagged, and it's just a short walk to the exit door of the store. Ahead of you is an aged man walking with a cane and an elderly woman beside him, pushing the grocery cart. God has obviously given them many years together. You think while you watch them cautiously move through the exit door that someday you might be like them. Worse, maybe you'll be all alone and returning home with groceries to an empty house. Turn that thought off, or the web might return with a spider that bleeds and consumes you.

The yummy warm chicken strips and waffle fries are now sitting on the passenger seat of your car. You can't wait to get home and, chances are, this morning's chores will be forgotten, and you'll never know if the lettuce hog needed a nice word from you. It could be that you missed a golden opportunity. She may have been taking her time because her eyes were dimmed by tears, standing there emotionally torn after learning that someone she loves received a terminal cancer report. Could you have been the smile she needed or the impromptu conversation that might have eased her heart? And that elderly couple that you passed up may have just visited their wounded warrior son's grave. Could you have found that out and told them how sorry you are and that you are thankful for their son's service? You could have offered to put their groceries into their car.

To be an ambassador for Jesus Christ, our antennas must be sensitive enough to pick up on instant opportunities. There's no room for cobwebs when a golden opportunity comes at a second's notice. If we wait for someone else to speak or act, we will be left as a skeleton covered with cobwebs. "Therefore encourage one another and build one another up . . . ." (1 Thessalonians 5:11)

There is an old saying that if there is dew on a spiderweb in the morning, the day will be beautiful. Take notice to see the sun pouring down upon dew-covered opportunities that sparkle like diamonds. Take notice that every day someone in your world, just a heartbeat from you, may need your hello, or your hand of help, or your ten-dollar bill placed in an outstretched hat. Grab the day and make beautiful history.

Discussion

Read James 1:5. Reflect on how wisdom and a keen sense of perception can help clean out the old cobwebs and help you grab golden opportunities to help others.

Take a few moments to reflect upon the words of Jesus in John 13:34. How might a loving spirit help, or quiet us in moments of irritation and anger?

God makes his appeal through us to be ambassadors for Christ. Read 2 Corinthians 5:20 and consider how this responsibility to represent Jesus to others can change your perspective on where you are right now.

Proverbs 28:1 says that the righteous are as bold as a lion. Lacking boldness is countered by the promise of God to help us brush off the cobwebs of timidity. Read 2 Timothy 1:7 and consider the power of the Holy Spirit to help you be an active ambassador for Jesus.

CHAPTER 6

The Sweet Smell of a Bonfire

The sweet, smoky smell of a bonfire is better than perfume for some people, because it brings memories of times sitting around a campfire with family and friends. The power of smell that provokes memories is known as the *Proust phenomenon*, and the scent of a bonfire can trigger emotionally rich recollections. Indeed, fire and smoke can trigger memories. I am reminded of an evening walk with my mother. Paul, her second husband, stayed back, saying he would get the fireplace started in the living room. That sounded like a good idea, because the cool night air was quickly moving in and there was enough chill that we needed to put on a jacket. When we returned from our walk, we found the doors and windows wide open and Paul was batting the air with a newspaper, trying the get the smoke out of the house. He had forgotten to open the damper. The house smelled far from Chanel N°5 Eau de Parfum. But aside from smoky fireplaces, the joy of a bonfire is the highlight of most campers. After a long day of pulling a travel trailer, the sight of an arrow pointing to a campground is almost as comforting as coming home to mom for supper. Eight hours of monotonous dotted road lines make the sight of a restful park an oasis. Campers know that after getting set up on the campsite and throwing a few logs on a campfire, the comfort feels as though engaging their primal instincts. The warmth of the flames and crackling sounds from the wood soothe the mind and body. There seems to be a multisensory experience when settling into a comfy canvas chair under a starlit sky, watching dancing flames light up the darkness. Nothing beats the woodsy, sweet fragrance of a campfire.

Speaking of fragrance, some time ago I was given a small piece of ivory-colored linen paper with beautiful hand-printed Italian italic words saying: "Mary—Blessed fragrance . . . a sweet wholesome fragrance in our lives." (2 Corinthians 2:15) I felt blessed and humbled while I read the message and felt the beautiful paper it was written on. I took joy in the meaning of the scripture, for it was solely about God in my life, not about me, and how I was to him the aroma of Christ, because I believed in Him. Yet another scripture says that Christ is a fragrant offering and sacrifice to us. (Ephesians 5:2) Indeed, the meanings of the Proust phenomenon are many. Truly, the sense of smell has bundles of meaningful history in it for us. Such as the scent of a live Christmas tree, the fragrance of a perfume that our mother wore, the pungent smell of our grandfather's cigar, and the trace of fresh-baked snickerdoodles filtering into the garage from the kitchen—all bringing back emotions. Even the scent on a soft blanket, taken from the mother dog after nursing her pup, is comforting to a pup who's been sold and has left the litter.

In the Hollywood movie *Scent of a Woman*, Lieutenant Colonel Frank Slade smells the scarf of the teacher who approaches him after his speech. He identifies her perfume as Fleur de Rocaille. That scene is remindful of my Aunt Betty who wore Bellodgia perfume by Caron. I'll bet you have never heard of it. Whenever I entered her house, the sweet aroma of her perfume struck a happy feeling. It was the Proust phenomenon, which is similar to that of beautiful music, having the power to tame the beast within us. The power of scent awakens both our past and present, and can prompt history-making opportunities. If you're a man reading this book, tomorrow might be a great history-making day if you come home to your wife with a dozen roses.

In comparison to the power of scent, the "airs" of human behavior undeniably produce history-making occasions and prompt both good and bad. Our personas might seem inconsequential, but surprisingly, they often reveal something powerful in our conduct that zooms straight into our future eternity, or someone else's. Without a hint that we have done anything of value or wrong, our effects on those we interface with may do something great or damaging.

Middle school age students—ages twelve to fourteen—are one of the hardest groups of children to work with because puberty is on the rampage in their bodies. I know this because my husband and I worked with this age group for several years at our church. We called these students *Alpha Teens*. Young girls this age are often ridiculously silly and emotional. Boys are simply awkward and unruly. There were times when I wanted to throw in the towel and quit. But near the end of each semester, I managed with dexterity and God's help to love each one, no matter how bad their behavior tried my patience.

The annual trips with each new group of adolescents to a beautiful lakepoint area near Traverse City, Michigan, for a long weekend of fun and spiritual enhancement were a rewarding once-a-year trip. Traditionally, the evening before we left the area for home, our planned agenda included building a bonfire and roasting s'mores. Graham crackers, marshmallows, and milk chocolate bars set the stage for humongous sugar highs, combined with their raging hormones. I knew no one would sleep those last nights, but my hope was that they might settle down and sleep during the four-hour trip back home the next day. Never! LOL.

Thinking back years later, the most important thing about the history-making impact on young junior high students was the Holy Spirit's influence on their young hearts and minds. I like to think that the bonfire was probably the best vehicle of impact and inspiration. Whatever was said during those evening hours under the starlit skies over Lake Michigan carried and lived on purposely in many of these Alpha Teens. Today, I see several of them as solid adult ambassadors for Christ. History was made within every new group, much of it to build the kingdom of God and reach far into eternity. I believe that bonfire moments happen in most everyone's life and, notoriously, some moments have permanent effects.

Just as the sweet smell of a bonfire is new when different logs are thrown into the flames, so is every new day. In a spiritual sense, the distinct smell of a bonfire, coupled with spangling flames, is like a person finding arrows pointing to opportunities that light new spiritual fires and allow our personal history to move on prolifically.

Discussion

Share some bonfire moments in your life that made lasting impressions on you. Discuss if there was a spiritual impact.

How do you see your life as a sweet fragrance of Christ, in reference to 2 Corinthians 2:15?

Read Ephesians 5:2 and consider how Christ is a fragrant offering and sacrifice to those who trust in him. Reflect on how His salvation offers a clean and fresh life to all who trust Him for salvation.

CHAPTER 7

Waiting in a Wilderness of Hope Is Often the Best Part

I n all the classrooms at Hutchinson Elementary School in Detroit, the narrow border across the top of the chalkboards spanned the entire wall behind the teacher's desk. Thumbtacked on those borders, the teachers posted colorful pictures of the upcoming holiday. Every child stared at those pictures with longing hearts, wanting the holiday to hurry up and come. Immediately after Thanksgiving, pictures of Santa, snowmen, horse-driven sleighs, and Christmas trees donned the borders. To a young child, the four-week wait for Christmas seemed as though it took ages to come, and their expectations grew.

On the adult flip side, life is not spent in childlike waiting, but in serious mixtures of happiness and death situations. For thought, picture the scenario of a head-on collision on a major expressway caused by an intoxicated person driving the wrong way. Someone is badly hurt, and their loved one is waiting with fear and anxiety for the ambulance to arrive. The wait is like the unrelenting ticking of the clock, running fast toward either life or death. Minutes seem like hours. Think of another situation: a pastor who spends hours on his knees praying for God to send the needed funds to keep the church running. His wait feels as though lost souls are eminently approaching eternity. Yet another person, in a different wilderness of waiting, longs for a child and prays earnestly that God will intervene. Year after year, the anxious want-to-be parents hope, while they watch other couples have children. To them, the wait feels like God is too busy to answer or is light-years away.

Waiting for something is a common element of life, gnawing at our patience, exciting every nerve in our body. We all know how nerve-racking the wait is on the phone for someone to get back on the line. The loud music playing into your ear sends us into maddening orbit, not to mention the constant injecting of a voice that says, *"Thanks for your patience."* Maybe worse is the degrading wait for the person who is always too busy to see you. Then there's the anxious wait for someone you have fallen in love with to pop the question.

Everyone waits for something, like maybe right now, you may be waiting anxiously for God to move on a situation that needs wisdom and help. Might it happen that waiting is the best part? Wait means *trust God.*

It was a cold February evening, many years ago, as I drove to Henry Ford Hospital in Detroit to be at my brother Robert's bedside. Glancing into my rearview mirror, I could see the sun slowly setting, its magnificent red and golden color sweeping across the western sky like the rhapsody of joy that was flooding my soul. Just minutes before, a telephone call from my sister-in-law was still ringing in my ears. Her voice was filled with hope and excitement. *"A heart just came in for Robert,"* she cried, *"they're prepping him now for the heart transplant!"* Seven long months of prayer and begging God to save my brother were now in the throes of being answered.

As I drove into the center of Detroit, I recalled an impacting message God placed in my heart several weeks earlier. It came to me on a Sunday afternoon as I sat in the intensive care unit visiting with Robert, my only sibling, who was terminally ill. The intensive care units at Henry Ford Hospital resembled prison cells to me that day. As a nurse, I knew well what happens in the sterile chambers of an ICU; lives often hang in the balance and death comes to many. A cold chill ran up my spine as I let this thought move into my mind.

My faith had been tried to the limit while I spent hours in prayer for my dying brother. Morbidity saturated my thoughts. I was exhausted from what seemed like a continuous wrestling match with God for my brother's life. I felt empty and defeated. Robert was suffering from acute cardiomyopathy. Back then, this deteriorating disease was one of the biggest killers of heart patients. The imminent threat of death was real for my brother, even though he miraculously survived several months of crisis episodes—all of them sending him back into the ICU again and again. The entire family was exhausted, as well as my hope for him to survive long enough to receive a heart transplant.

As I sat at his bedside that Sunday afternoon, I seemed to sense a morbid presence, like that of the death angel hovering close by. Robert had that *look* that every nurse knew, and I was scared. But then, while I sat watching him, a silent message came straight out of the blue into my grieving heart. Strange, how it interrupted my morbidity and called me to attention. It was one of those moments that Christians talk about, when God's Spirit comes so close that you can almost touch Him. You know He is speaking. I felt a powerful stillness come over my soul. It wasn't actual words that I heard, but I understood what was being said to me. The message drove a spear through every tormenting doubt I had. It cut straight into my doubting heart. The voice said, *"No matter what you see and how critical your brother is, I want you to wait patiently and keep trusting me."*

It was God's Spirit talking. Tears came to my eyes. *Wait*, the Spirit said to me. That's all I was doing for the last several months—waiting and praying like a lawyer fighting against a death sentence for their client. Trust? I was trusting the best I knew how. For seven months, I watched my brother slowly deteriorate and barely escape death. Many times, his heart team worked frantically into the long hours of the night to keep him alive. How can a person truly trust when death seems just hours away? How much longer, God? Those were the questions hanging in the balance. I was challenging God to make up His mind. Yet in that strange and unique quietness, sitting next to Robert in that sterile ICU bed, the message was clear. I knew the answer God would give, one way or the other. His answer would not be simply for the sake of my brother's life or my persistent prayers, but it would glorify God in some way. Time out here! Do you get this? God's answers are not for anyone's personal sake, but for the glory of God in some way.

The entire cardiac department knew Robert, the brave one awaiting a heart transplant. Nurses on other floors heard about him and would come to meet him, some just to get a glimpse. He was a curious challenge to everyone's thinking of life and death. He was there so long that he became the main challenge to every doctor and every nurse who attended him. Robert was their courageous fighter who kept hanging on. His spirit of hope was in play every day. Surely, I could be the same for his sake. That Sunday afternoon, I went home inspired, yet greatly concerned that the outcome I wanted would not be given.

On the other side of the Motor City, hidden within its noise and clamor, an accidental shooting happened. The life of an eighteen-year-old teenager was unintentionally snuffed out when his gun went off accidentally and sent a bullet into his head. The surgeons worked unsuccessfully to save his life. Strange it was, yet miraculous how this moment played out. Robert lay waiting for a miracle while the boy's grieving mother found the courage to release his organs. His young heart was a perfect match for my dying brother.

In the providence of God, which is often impossible to understand, one family was immediately plunged into grief, while another family was filled with hope. It happens every day. Organ transplants come from the dead to save the living. On this day in my brother's history, a teenager died, and his heart gave life to my brother. Robert lived for twelve more years, and the glory of God was evidenced by all who knew him. Of course, I was relieved and grateful to God. But the heart transplant did not entirely play out to satisfy human longings, but for the evidence of God's mysterious ways to bring glory to His name. I still stood at his casket twelve years later and wept. I'm sure Mary and Martha wept for Lazarus when he died years later, after Jesus raised him from the dead. Who can figure any of this out, but simply to know that God will get his glory? Jesus said, "If we will not give God the glory due to Him, the stones in the sidewalk will rise up and give it."

Indeed, the wait for Robert's heart transplant was terrible to endure, but looking back, I knew that the hours I spent alone with God and at Robert's side were spiritual gold. Waiting in a wilderness of hope built my faith to a higher level. It changed many things into proper perspectives. In the shadowy desert, where waiting touches the core of our faith, we look back on life and the history we've been making and see God's hand and purpose.

We must wait for God, long and meekly, in the wind and wet, in the thunder and lightning, in the cold and dark, wait, and He will come. He never comes to those who do not wait. (Fr. Frederick William Faber, English hymn writer and theologian, 1814 - −1863.)

On a sidenote about prayer, a person may ask why do we get other people praying for us? In a Sunday school class some time ago, a lady asked this daunting question: Why does it take so many people to get God to do something—isn't one prayer enough? Great question. How many times must you ask for the saltshaker sitting in front of the person across the table? Once, because he hears your request and he shoves the shaker over to you. So then, are prayer chains and large groups of people praying performed to convince God to answer? If the saltshaker is in front of God, so to speak, and He owns it and has the power to pass it, wouldn't one request be enough? Yes. Most likely, the person with one prayer, and wringing wet with faith, has no need to get fifty more praying people. So, logically and spiritually, we can pray once and then wait. And sometimes, I want to do just that.

Cannot the "wait" that Father William Faber writes about be the point of absolute faith for all of us? In truth, the spiritual point of praying for others is this: Collective praying gives unity and strengthens the community of believers with a shared sense of purpose. And for the person who is waiting, simply knowing others are praying aids in calming anxiety and worry. While another person says, I pray alone. I wait alone. Either way, God answers. So, take your pick.

Waiting and hope go together. To poet Emily Dickinson, *"Hope" is the thing with feathers.* Her pen said it *perches in the soul* of the person who is hoping and *sings the tune without words*, and it *never stops*. Emily wrote that hope is the *chillest land* to be in and concluded wistfully that it lingers *on the strangest Sea; yet never in Extremity did it ask a crumb of me*. In other words, hope is eternal and always present. So, save your crumbs and keep hoping.

Discussion

Read Proverbs 3:5–6. Consider the paths that God might make for you as you wait and trust Him. Can spiritual gain happen while waiting for answers? How?

In I Chronicles 28:3, King David's desire to build the temple was given to his son Solomon. Consider how other people receive what we pray for, and we are left out. How should we feel when we regard the sovereignty of God in everything we pray for and hope for?

Read 2 Corinthians 12:7–10. What was Paul's attitude when God did not answer his prayer regarding the thorn in his flesh? Contemplate how God's grace is sufficient in weakness.

CHAPTER 8

We're Never Too Old

Shut the front door and grab a comfy seat, because this chapter is for you if you think you're too old to do something spectacular. It's not a stretch of the imagination to think that every stage of life has possibilities to build a new platform, even in the golden years. All of us are history in the making every day.

Can you guess what is considered the age to start feeling old? According to the Worldwide Independent Network of Market Research, 43 is a good answer. I can agree, except that I didn't "feel" old at that age, but I definitely hated to see my 40th birthday come. I wanted to stay 39 for the rest of my life. When a friend of mine turned gray during her forties, she said she earned every one of those hairs. I notice that everyone ages differently, the same as everyone acts differently. It is my opinion that the most beautiful people are not those with porcelain skin and perfect figures, but those who have faced horrendous problems and come through like stars. Every one of us walks through our own storms—and it's true that stress shows up in physical ways—but when we emerge with the wind at our back and gain more appreciation for life, we move forward and grab the next opportunity. No matter how old a person gets, if there's life and spark, a new manifesto is waiting.

For instance, take Colonel Harland Sanders, the creator and founder of Kentucky Fried Chicken. He gained momentum and success when KFC went public on the New York Stock Exchange in 1969. He was 79 years old at the time. More than 3,500 franchised and company-owned restaurants were in worldwide operation when Heublein Inc. acquired the KFC Corporation in 1971, for a grand total of 285 million. PepsiCo, Inc. now owns the company for a net worth of $205.19 billion. Yum! Finger licking good! Sanders made world history for himself and chicken.

Too old? Never!

From poor to riches are other stories that tell that a dream and hard work can bring success and even make you rich. It seldom happens in childhood. Take for instance Steve Jobs. He was adopted and dropped out of college, but he cofounded Apple and revolutionized the personal computer industry. There are hundreds of other stories of wild ideas becoming worldwide phenomenon. Not just in business, but in family life, community life, and human relationships. The most remarkable of all commitments is to follow Jesus Christ. Hundreds of well-known people have become Christians and sincerely committed their lives to Christ. It's not just us peons who know that the most lucrative decision in life to make is to commit your life to Christ. The list of well-knowns include Stephen Baldwin, Kirk Cameron, George W. Bush, Alice Cooper, Chuck Norris,

Brian "Head" Welch—the rock guitarist of Korn, and George Foreman, just to name a few.

Too late? Never!

It's never too late for a dream, as well as never too late for a deathbed moment, to settle the question of eternal life. Many famous people have made deathbed commitments to Christ—for example, John Wayne, Oscar Wilde, Charles II of England, just to start the list. One of the most publicly prized death-bed conversions was one whose showy character was known as "King of Cool." That would be actor Steve McQueen. Before McQueen's cancer diagnosis, he had little thought of being a Christian. When he became gravely ill, he requested to meet with Billy Graham, who, you will recall, was a former world-renowned evangelist. Graham flew to meet him at the airport before McQueen's final surgery in Mexico. Their meeting resulted in Graham leading McQueen to salvation in Jesus Christ. Before leaving the meeting and flying back home, Graham handed McQueen his personal crusade Bible. Four days later, McQueen died clutching the Bible. He was fifty years old.

As God keeps giving us life, every stage has a platform on which our existence can build. A commitment to follow Jesus Christ is the only solid platform of peace and assurance of eternal life. The Bible says we become new creatures in Christ Jesus when we accept Him as our Lord and Savior. Second Corinthians 5:17 says that we who are following Christ become the new creatures and the old things pass away and all things become new. A new door opens up, and our personal history is fresh and pristine. We do not have to create a worldwide fried chicken restaurant chain to be history-successful with Jesus. And forget about thinking that you're the worst sinner that ever lived and God can't rescue you. He can, and He has done it for millions of people. The apostle Paul, for one, whom I featured in a previous chapter. Paul persecuted the Church, and after his conversion, he claimed that he was chief of all sinners. Yet, his history shows he was one of the most acclaimed Christians the world has known—sinner or not. Forget about age and sin. Age has nothing to do with salvation and success. It's simply realizing that God has a plan for your life, and history is waiting to be made. Seek the plan. Make history. Consider the exhortation of Philippians 4:13, "I can do all things through Christ who strengthens me."

Here's one special nugget for me and anyone else who wants to write or do anything past the age of 50 (not that I am 50 years old. I'm more. It's just a benchmark). Harry Bernstein started writing his first novel, *The Invisible Wall: A Love Story That Broke Barriers*, when he was 93 years old. Three years later, in 2007, it was published at the age of 96, and he gained literary fame. He went on to write other books. He died at the age of 101 in 2011.

The bottom line is that our life is making history every day. I've already mentioned that in just two generations we will likely be forgotten. So, if personal history means anything, it means that we need to grab hold of the opportunities staring us in the face and make a good mark. In the end, when the books are open and our history is reviewed, the best words we could hear will be, *Well done!*

Discussion

What dream or future plans have you been thinking about? How might you begin to make it happen? Jot down the pros and cons, and meditate on how you can bring it to life.

How would you define Philippians 4:13? Does it encourage faith to believe that whatever difficulty or weakness we encounter, we can gain success?

Think of someone you know who has gained great success and consider how they were able to achieve their goal. Would their method be of encouragement to you? If so, how could you incorporate it to work for you?

CHAPTER 9

What People Want Most

What one person says they desire most in life may be entirely opposite of what another deems most important, but when focused on the essential realities, it is love that is most wanted. I am referring to the innermost being of a person, such as one's inner self or spirit. Of course, people with serious mental conditions may have all sorts of answers, but for the grand majority of human beings, love is desired as the most-wanted thing in life. So, I asked AI if all humans want love, because it seemed to make sense to me that everyone is born with an intrinsic need for it. I know I need love! Here is the answer I got, generated across the web and in Google's Knowledge Graph: *Yes, universally, people have a fundamental need for love and belonging. This need is considered a core human need, essential to both individual and collective survival. Psychologists and other experts have shown that love is crucial for mental and physical well-being.* So, acknowledging that this is true, it seems understandable that Jesus strongly clarified that the second most important commandment is to love your neighbor as yourself. (Matthew 22:39)

Most of us enjoy a good love story, and there are plenty of them out there. It seems that God's plan of procreation had to have some sort of love in it, otherwise the world would not have well over eight billion people living today. My uncle Bernard and his wife Beulah (who have since departed this world over forty years ago) fascinated me as a kid. They were two lovebirds showing outward affection for each other in front of me, as though they had a mysterious chemistry that caused them to kiss and hold hands in public. They had no children, which I found sad because my uncle was an adopted child who never connected with his blood family. My dad and he enjoyed being stepbrothers, and that's another story. Many times, I thought it would be wonderful if Uncle Bernard could have a son or daughter to call his very own. I felt sorry for him, even though Beulah loved him dearly.

They lived in Flint, Michigan, and on rare occasions, they traveled to our house in Detroit to visit. I was quite young, but I remember these lovebirds sitting on our couch, holding hands, and telling a story about the flame on their furnace pilot light going out in midwinter. I can still picture them, snuggled close and Aunt Beulah enhancing the story with her deep contralto voice. Both of them feared that the furnace might blow up when a lighted match was held close to the pilot—of course, with the gas flowing from it. They determined that if an explosion occurred, they would want to die together. I listened with intrigue, thinking that the next part of the story would be that the furnace blew up and the basement became a fireball of flames. It seemed to my childish imagination that a blown-out pilot light on a furnace was a life-threatening situation. But Uncle Bernard was smiling and squeezing Aunt Beulah's hand, so I knew if they had an explosion, it had not leveled their house or hurt them. With a lighted match in one hand and holding Aunt Beulah's hand with the other, he touched the match flame to the pilot. It lit perfectly. Wow, I thought, they really must love each other to want to die together. Their love for each other made an impression on me that has lasted more than forty years after their deaths. They made family history for all of us.

Love, when viewed as a drive such as hunger, thirst, sleep, or sex, would be an indifferent interpretation, because it is treating it as a mere motive. Love is more than that. It is characterized by affection, desire, and promise, or vow.

Not all forms of love are the same, and psychologists have identified different types of love that people experience. Love for your spouse is different from the love you have for your mother or father. Love for your child is different from love for a sister or brother. Even biblical love is defined as *agape*, meaning godly love, and that's another, different love.

Searching about love further, I found it interesting that social psychologist Zick Rubin created a scale from liking to loving, to show the differences between close feelings and love. He claimed three elements in actual love: (1) *Attachment*, which means to be cared for and to be with the other person; (2) *Caring*, which encompasses valuing the other person's happiness as much as your own; and, (3) *Intimacy*, which means sharing your private thoughts, feelings, and desires with the other person.

I am in love as I write this. I married again after having a long and wonderful marriage with my first husband, who sadly passed away a few years ago. My new marriage sometimes feels surreal. As though I walked through a new door, and all was fresh and even strange at times. Love has many different feelings. I recognize, however, that the actual elements of love are the same regardless of how it comes about. Attachment, caring, and intimacy mean that love has no dissimilarities. My feelings for my new partner encompass love and liking, just as they did with my first husband. Personalities are different, but the elements and emotions and feelings of love are the same.

My parents were not kissy-face-huggy-bear people. Actually, I cannot remember them kissing in front of me. Papa loved Mama, and Mama loved Papa, but I never saw physical evidence. I only saw a little of that in the John Wayne Westerns when he hugged the cowgirl at the end of the movie. When I was eleven years old, I saw what looked like love. My parents invited a young couple to spend a weekend with us in our cottage at Port Sanilac. Phyllis and Ronnie. We didn't have a spare bedroom or bed to accommodate them, so the men (my brother, Robert included) decided to sleep in a tent and let the ladies have the beds. After supper, we sat outdoors enjoying the sound of Lake Huron waves rush up on shore and watching the hundreds of stars filling the sky. When bedtime came, my eyes bugged out of my head when Ronnie took Phyllis into his arms and they kissed and stood in a tight embrace for what seemed like forever. I think his hand reached down over her rump, and I thought maybe I should run into the house. Then I heard him say to her, "I'll miss you." I didn't know what was coming next, but I wasn't going to miss it. If this was love, I had to see it.

For as long as this couple stayed in my parents' lives, I saw these two lovebirds show physical love for each other whenever we were together. I got used to seeing them kiss and touch each other, and I knew that I wanted to be just like Phyllis and have that kind of love when I grew up and got married.

The greatest love of all is the love that God has for each of us. His love is summed up in the gospel of John 3:16–17: "For God so loved the world, that he gave his only begotten Son, that whosoever believes in him should not perish but have everlasting life. For God sent not his Son into the world to condemn the world; but that the world through him might be saved."

If you have never accepted Jesus as your Savior, now is the time to do so. God loves you and is waiting for you to put your faith and trust in Him.

Discussion

How has a love relationship changed your life?

Recall a memory of someone you considered enjoying a loving relationship with and think about how their influence made you feel. What was the inward effect upon you, especially if you were in search of love?

Think about the people in your life who need to experience the love of God. How might you witness to them of God's love? Pray for God to show you how to approach them.

CHAPTER 10

The Critical Failing Church

I want to be honest and assertively upfront that I love the Church and its people. The core of this chapter reflects my sorrow regarding the recognizable turning away from biblical precepts and principles in many churches and denominations today. The Bible warns that in the Last Days before Christ returns to earth, a great falling away from God will happen, and sadly, it seems to include the Christian Church. Let me quote the warning: *"Now brethren, concerning the coming of our Lord Jesus Christ and our gathering together to Him, we ask you not to be soon shaken in mind or troubled, either by spirit or by word or by letter, as if from us, as though the day of Christ had come. Let no one deceive you by any means, for that Day will not come unless the falling away comes first, and the man of sin is revealed, the son of perdition [the antichrist], who opposes and exalts himself above all that I called God of that I worshiped . . . ."* (2 Thessalonians 2:1–4, NKJV) We are clearly seeing a significant departure from Christianity and its holy traditions in our culture and society, as well as the Church.

Easing my sorrow somewhat about the turning away of Gospel truth in many churches is my pleasant view of Africa and the entire Global South, for I learned that, regardless of the apologetic state of Christianity in the United States, the gospel of Jesus Christ is flourishing there. In various parts of Africa, Christianity has grown to six million Christians, almost double the number documented in 2010. Nigeria is the phenomenal exception, growing by 50.8% in this period. It is heartbreaking that the United States is experiencing a noticeable shift away from Christian identity, showing a staggering decline in church attendance, as has been reported by the Pew Research Center. The shift away from God and righteous living has been observed by many noted Christian ministers. Years ago, Ruth Graham, the wife of evangelist Billy Graham, is quoted as saying, "If God doesn't punish America, He will have to apologize to Sodom and Gomorrah."[1]

The Christian Church is in warfare on two fronts: a battle against the progressive culture's attitude about God, and an overall pulling away from biblical precepts and holy traditions of its leaders and members. Proof of this is substantiated by the copious changes in style of worship and message content that are taking place even in the most fundamental churches. Much of this warfare is driven by multiple advancements in technology, which erase the holy beauty of the worship exercise.

Indeed, the enemies of the Christian Church are everywhere, even in Artificial Intelligence (AI) as it invades our smartphones, our services of digital assistants, chatbots, and

---

1 Sojourners, solo.net

social media websites. You will find AI in robot vacuum cleaners, security systems, and in your auto-navigation system, just to cite a few more places. The bottom line is that AI and the mainstream culture are changing everything everywhere, even in the local church you and I attend. As technology and social conduct change, the impacts upon traditional principles and precepts of worship are being altered and even abandoned. Worse, the gospel of Jesus Christ is suffering. This should never be happening. The counteraction for the Church in this warfare is to take an unwavering stand that the gospel message of Jesus Christ is forever and unchangeable. It needs no created systems or frenzied marketing strategies to enhance it.

The sad truth is that the Christian Church is surrendering to the culture bullies, and is engaging in a marketing fury that shifts its traditions and evangelical impact to a come-as-you-are, get comfy, and rest in watered-down versions of salvation in Jesus Christ. In simple words, the Church is hanging and clicking with the world, in many churches in America and around the world. It is not wholly in sync with God and the power of the Holy Spirit. Instead, it is changing its language and trading its dignity and spiritual commitment for AI technology and social acceptance. I said earlier that I wanted to be honest and assertively upfront, so maybe it's time to say bring back the choir, play the bells of the organ, read from a literal Bible, and readopt the holy traditions. What gives me this courage to challenge the failing Church is found in 2 Thessalonians 2:15, which says to stand firm and cling to the traditions we have been taught and hold to the importance of the teachings of Jesus Christ.

As we look back just twenty-five years, we can ascertain that the world has undergone many major changes, and a new breed of humans has arisen. A statement from AI, which I obtained from a Google search on the diverse segments of our population as seen through the lens of biblical truth, principles, and values, offers this: *Only 7% of Gen X have a biblical view. Millennials have a lesser biblical view of 6%, while just a mere 4% of Gen Z have a biblical view.* So, as anxious pastors and leaders in the Church worry about declining attendance, they authorize copious marketing strategies to increase attenders. Whoa! Here is the crux of the problem. Their ideology for increased attendance is based on pleasing the culture, rather than depending on the power that is in the gospel itself. Proof of this is in many churches where they have transitioned from choir-led, melody-rich music to unfamiliar songs and monotonous lyrics that repeat and repeat the same words, plus totally relaxed and undignified worship. It's a setup that hints at mainstream style and liberal societal behaviors.

I'm not saying that there are pot smokers lighting up on the steps of the premises, or flag-wavers in the pews, but I'm citing that the Christian Church is allowing careless behavior to accommodate the trends of the culture. Sloppy jeans, shorts, and flip flops are common attire from the practice of dressing in respect of the King of kings. The choirs and solos have been yanked out of the service, and sippy coffee cups have become the norm for those adult babies who cannot sit for one hour without something in their mouth. All that's missing in some sanctuaries are the ants from the picnic table, or the warm beer left over from the ballgame. The organ is out and drums and guitars are in—which is okay, but sometimes a stretch for holy worship.

Unfortunately, all this leniency is not growing the Church, and that's my point. The Church has also become Big Brother in many ways, capturing much of the precious time families should have with their members. Their ideas are similar to the seized authority within the public school system, which is caught up in meeting what they believe are the "felt needs" of children and their parents.

Likewise, many churches have two separate gatherings on Sunday morning. Worship is split into two different worship services and time frames, labeled *Traditional* and *Contemporary*. Traditional service is known as the *congregation of the old guard*, or those who hold true to the order and holiness of the long-established traditions of the church. Leaders who take part in both services are known to change clothes from one service to another to suit the tailored styles of the attenders. What has emerged from the decision to hold two services is two separate churches under one roof. It's hard to love the brethren because half the church does not know the other half. A clear division has been made, and the line drawn in this division interferes with agape, brotherly love. Moreover, this division also introduces a sad sense of loneliness in many attenders. (Refer to chapter 3, Only the Lonely.)

The Christian Church is busy building its twenty-first-century platform. Taking it into an honest spotlight and contrasting it with the conservative and spiritual attitudes fifty years ago, it is clear that the panache of the Church is now geared to making people feel comfy, rather than attending a dignified worship service and hearing sermons that preach about both sin and salvation. Inviting attenders to accept Christ as their Savior is now a lost practice in many church denominations. Feeling good and hearing no controversial words that challenge social, moral, or political ideology is the new marketing strategy. It suggests that pastors must cautiously sermonize the Bible and not use it to challenge sin or politics. And so, the history of the Church has changed to become a person's experience of freedom instead of the actual truth from the Bible about Jesus Christ and Him crucified. It is fast losing its power to preach against sin and lead its attenders to salvation. It is fast losing its hallowed influence to lead its congregation into reverent, holy, dignified worship. The ideology running the Sunday worship service is to assure its attenders of feeling good and hearing no polemic words that might bring controversy about social, moral, or political ideology. The watchword appears to be: *Never specifically call out sin.* Never say the words *sex, homosexual, abortion, transsexual, drug user, wife abuser, and pornography*, etc. Do these avoidances benefit growth? I greatly challenge that it does not benefit the Church, and there is data to claim that I am right.

Recent AI research claims that 62% of churches have no growth or their congregations are declining. COVID is not the prime reason that people left the church and why they are not returning. The reason is that we have the prophetic fulfilment of a great falling away, with strong enemies of the soul hard at work to destroy the Church. Strange it is, but always expected, that churches are packed on Christmas and Easter. This is primarily due to the joy and happiness of the message on those two holidays. Let me sound the trumpet here and say that the good news of a loving God and a Savior that saves and forgives could pack the churches again. But only if this good news is preached every Sunday without a bunch of weird tricks, like expository preaching of certain hand-picked parts of the Bible and then, two or three minutes about Jesus and saving grace. Sunday morning sermons resembling Bible studies or prosperity lectures are not interesting to people coming to church to worship God or helpful in finding solid answers for a sinner's problems. The big bang of life is in the forgiving blood of Jesus Christ. I'm a nurse, and I know that life is in the blood. That's one of the first things I learned. The first procedure a doctor asks for is a blood profile. What's wrong with a person will show up in the blood analysis. Life is in the blood. Life is in the shed blood of Jesus. Lifeless sermons that mimic Bible studies or strive to simply tickle attenders' ears with happy-go-lucky speeches that promise God will give them everything they want do not bring people back. Pastors who give false promises to those seeking to be saved are far from the truth when they emphasize the belief that God will bless followers with wealth and success in return for their faith. No one can earn salvation. It's a gift of God to those who believe in Jesus Christ and take Him as their Savior. There's no scriptural promise that once you become a follower of Jesus Christ, your path is headed for the gold at the end of the rainbow. The promise is that sins are forgiven and eternal life is assured. What more would a person want than relief from the guilt of sin and the promise to never die?

The crisis in the Christian Church, likewise, is having to deal with the lack of young adult attenders and financial support. This, sadly, is an honest and major problem. However, the spiritual breakdown is not simply the absence of attenders and money but is often linked to the unwise choices made by its leaders. Leaders add and delete things on impulse to draw people in, and essentially, they cater to the notion that the gospel needs human help. They change style, message, and program to stay in tune and in touch with mainstream ideology and the mores of the up-to-the-minute culture. Young attenders are all of this, but to reel them into the church takes more than style. So, leaders assure themselves wrongly that their decisions will bring in young adult attenders with families and money. It's not turning out that way, instead, it's helping cripple the Church more.

It should not come as a surprise to those who have their head up and out of the sand and are tuned to world news that Satan is working hard to destroy both the Church and Christians. It's time that Christians lead into battle. The front-runners of the church, those spearheads that have been ordained into high positions, need to understand that there's nothing more powerful than the message of Jesus Christ and His saving grace. It does not need drummed-up human help. All the antics of coaxing attenders to feel comfy and giving them free will do not save them, let alone bring them back. A cup of coffee and a doughnut given in the entrance hall of the church, along with a wink of the eye saying it is fine to take your sippy cup to the pew, is not going to capture them. An empty choir loft and loud drums and guitars will not lead a person to Jesus. The power of the gospel is what will save them and bring them back. Preach this, dear pastors, and let God work!!!

I've struggled with this chapter; I even thought of deleting it. But I truly believe it's time to recognize that God is still in His Holy temple and the Christian Church needs to bow before Him. It's time that the gospel message of Jesus Christ is preached with Holy Spirit gumption, and with it an invitation to receive Him. It's time to use the talents within the congregation to beautify the message and affirm the gifts that God has given to His people. It's time to stop all the nonsense of culture-friendly antics and simply showcase Jesus. The lost and hungry will come. Yes, they will come if the Church presents Jesus Christ in all His beauty and power.

Christians, let us say this: "... *[We are] not ashamed of the gospel of Christ, for it is the power of God unto salvation to everyone who believes, to the Jew first and also to the Greek* [gentiles]. *For in it the righteousness of God is revealed . . . .*" (Romans 1:15–17, NKJV)

Discussion

Do you believe the Church is experiencing a falling away from God and His precepts and principles? If so, why? If not, why?

Do you see changes in the message and style of worship? If so, do you believe the changes have brought new attenders or have had no noticeable effect?

Can you relate or agree with 2 Thessalonians 2:1–4 that the world and the Church are experiencing a great falling away from God? If so, how are you seeing it?

We're Nearing the End

I t's no secret that the world has become increasingly evil as each decade goes by. Political posturing worldwide is adding up to the reality of the End, as a study of biblical prophecy reveals. Exactly as Christ spoke and was quoted by Matthew, Mark, and Luke well over two thousand years ago, the world is drowning in evil. The Bible gives many clues to watch for and, with surety, we can quote Christ and believe Him when He warned, "When you see these things happening, take heed, for the End is near." (Matthew 24) The list of things is accurate to the letter, except for the physical reign of the antichrist. As Christ sat upon the Mount of Olives, His disciples came to Him and asked Him when the End of the world would come. His answer is called the *Olivet Discourse*.

The format and history of the present day Church is rapidly changing. The list of things in the Olivet Discourse is an undebatable truth, accurately citing everything we are experiencing at this time in world history. Christ told the disciples that there will be wars and rumors of wars, —terrible atrocities committed—religious deceivers—hundreds of false truth in books on the market and available on Kindle—kingdoms at odds with each other—famines, and pestilences. COVID is the last warning, but more to come—and copious earthquakes documented every day. These things are just the beginning. Jews, and Christians alike, will be tormented and distressed, along with Christian martyrs slain every day. AI overviews of martyrs in the twenty-first century vary, but some sources suggest around 100,000 Christians were killed each year between 2000 and 2010. It is staggering to estimate how many more have been killed in the last fourteen years. Anyone believing in Jesus, when the End finally comes in full force, will be hated. People will be quick-tempered and ready to lash out and betray one another. Brother against brother, sister against sister, and children against their parents. I know this to be true, for when I spoke godly truth against sin in my family, members came against me and even lied against me. False religious leaders and teachers will take advantage of people who attend church and deceive them with words from the pulpit. The love of many will wax cold. It's happening as I write and as you read this book.

The coming of a Golden Age for America has been announced by the conservative media. President Donald Trump promises to bring a new golden age. The evil leaders of the past have supposedly been thrown in the dumpster. We see them licking their wounds and salivating to destroy every hope of a new golden age. Evil is as evil does, so they continue to do everything in their power to stop the good that a new golden age might bring. If Trump can reshape the nation, I'll be the first to salute him. My guess, however, is that it will take more than Trump to get our country under sane authority. We need a miracle from God.

What helps to bring a good sense of peace to those of us of Christian faith is that we know God is in control and He is moving forward with His agenda to bring Christ back. We know the Bible does not lie. In the New Testament writings of the apostle Paul, we find him giving a list of evils, just as Christ did. He left no stone unturned. He seems to shout, as his pen writes with intensity in 2 Timothy 3. I'm interpreting his list as he penned it and giving credence in detail. Terrible times are coming. The great majority of people will be totally narcissistic, loving themselves and jealous of others, while boasting about how great they are. Indeed, Paul has it perfectly correct. This is our world today. As I studied the subject of End-time prophecy, I found that every Bible translation has all sorts of adjectives to describe what Paul was warning about. My conclusion is that the next trumpet sound of God will be the return of Christ for His Church.

The list goes on. Abusive. Disobedient to parents. Unforgiving. Slanderous and without self-control. Now to the grand finale and the greatest evil of all—people loving pleasure rather than being lovers of God. In other words, having a form (or style) of godliness, but denying its power. This is why America is no longer considered a Christian nation.

Could all this evil mean that the End is imminent? I say a loud, *yes*, because the posture of the world has only one major benchmark to achieve: the rule of the antichrist. I would not hesitate to say that everything is also in place for the mystery event of the Rapture. This event is the instantaneous snatching away of Christians to meet with Christ in heaven. The account of this is in 1 Corinthians 15:51 - 53. Allow me to relate it. Paul's letter to the Corinthians told of a mystery event that was going to happen. He said not everyone will die, but they shall be changed in a moment, like in the twinkling of an eye. This will happen at what is called *the last trumpet sound of God*. This event, called the *Rapture*, says the dead in Christ shall rise from their graves incorruptible, and the Christians who are alive shall be immediately changed to meet Christ in the air and be with Him in heaven. Therefore, the Rapture of living Christians and the restoration of dead Christians all at the same time is called the *Resurrection*.

We are assured by everyday happenings that evil never takes a nap. It schemes and moves forward perpetually, and the accounts of it are sickening. One horrible escalation was on October 7, 2023, when Hamas poured into southern Israel and committed genocide in Israel. It is monstrous and repulsive that many around the world cheered Hamas, because the crimes that were committed are too gruesome to even think about, let alone write about them.

On March of 2025, Islamic radicals pushed their way into Syria, where non-Alawite religious minorities live, including Christians, and were targeted and killed. Many from these groups fled their villages to the mountains. While this factual event happened, it is important to note that the situation is complex in the Middle East, and different groups and factions are involved. Thus, Jesus was telling the truth when He said we would hear of wars and rumors of war. I relate the words of Isaiah 5:20: It refers to those who distort moral codes and cause wars by saying evil is good. The prophet writes, "Woe to all those who are calling evil good, and those who turn light into darkness. Misery also to people who put bitter for sweet." In other words, it is abominably shameful of those who distort the truth and deliberately confuse good with evil and vice versa.

It is not just in the Middle East; and throughout other parts of the world, that we have sickening levels of evil. The ravaging of hell on earth is here in the United States, attributed to years of open borders for all criminals and those with hateful attitudes against Israel and the Jews. We lock our doors, install security systems, carry a gun in our car or purse, and have security men manning guns in our churches. Never in any of our lifetimes have we seen such levels of evil causing us to defend ourselves with locks, cameras, and guns.

As I write this, enemies throughout the world are engaged in their most insane and expansive conflicts in decades, excluding World War I and World War II. Most concerning is that they may expand into using new tools of war, including nuclear weapons. The United States is securing and tightening up to such a point that many believe World War III is about to begin. The world has been warned in the Bible that wars and rumors of war will be constantly threatening, and evil will rise to such a level that there will be no peace on earth anywhere. Africa is experiencing several armed conflicts. The people in Ukraine have no peace. The war between Ukraine and Russia has killed thousands and destroyed many beautiful buildings. There is no golden age for the world.

Truly, the posture of the world has set the stage for the End. How much worse can it get before evil completely implodes the planet? I quote from the newsletter of the minister Jan Markell, *Understanding the Times*, Spring 2025 issue. A journalist wrote to her and said, "We are living in some kind of bizarro *Twilight Zone* episode or a zombie apocalypse nightmare." Markell responded, "No, we are not in a twilight zone or an apocalypse nightmare; rather, it is the last days and we should expect this."

Someday a mysterious silence may envelope the entire atmosphere. Silence —a peculiar silence in your house or the room you sleep in. In other places of the world, the same silence. In the twinkling of an eye, every true believer in Christ Jesus will be raptured, taken up. The long prophesied and predicted event that people laugh about and say would never happen, will take place. Bibles will remain on the shelves and the nightstands. Their words, still alive, still breathing the truth of God. It will be too late for the lost, unless they defy the evil rulers of the world and the antichrist, who will quickly come upon the scene. It won't be easy to find God when this happens.

The past cannot be retrieved. The good and the bad in our lives will never be ours again. What we do today is history in immediate making. And that's a good thing, because the present is what belongs to each of us. Each day we live is new. What happens with what we have control of depends upon us. Remember September 11, 2001, when the New York World Trade Center was attacked. Churches around the world and here in America, from east and west, north to south, churches were filled the following Sunday with people turning their attention to God. Suddenly, everyone was getting religion. America experienced a Jesus moment. Days later, however, only those who worked to clear the rubble and bury the dead were still praying. The nation went back to its narcissistic behavior, filling their stomachs, dulling their minds with strong drink and drugs, enjoying selfish pleasure, and not giving God a thought. New York City survived, but spiritually, it went back to its sinful ways. We have also survived COVID to a great extent, but again, we are a nation avoiding God's precepts and principles. Could there be another catastrophe, and would it shake us to repent?

The Church is still here, weak as it seems, but the gates of hell are not prevailing against it. There are still millions of Christians following Christ. We are the Church, and a sovereign God is very much in control. He allows and restrains at His will, while He moves His agenda forward to Christ's return. Friend, keep on building your history in a good way each day, regardless of what you see and hear. Don't get discouraged. Grab that new platform you have been dreaming about. Take hold of that project you promised to complete. Do that special thing that has been incubating in your mind and heart. As God gives life, occupy!

Discussion

Have you experienced some of the things Christ mentioned in Matthew 24? If so, what are they? Are you convinced that the world is near the End?

Do you believe America can have a new golden age of prosperity and peace? What convinces you either way?

Is there hope for peace in the Middle East? If so, how do you believe it will happen?

We have much control over our lives and how we live our present history each day. What would you change in your life, knowing Christ's return is imminent? Why would you make changes?

CHAPTER 12

The Phenomenal Plan

The good news is that God did not leave us in a doomed predicament. God provided a rescue plan by giving His Son, Jesus Christ, as the sacrifice for the sins of mankind and thus provide reconciliation between God and man. With this provision also comes the gift of eternal life. "The gift of God is eternal life in Christ Jesus our Lord." (Romans 6:23b)

God's plan of salvation is phenomenal as well as simple to understand. It took place long before you and I were born (or anyone for that matter), when God recognized in His infinite wisdom—which goes beyond measure or comprehension—that His human creation would need a plan of salvation. His plan was an unmerited gift to us because He knew from the beginning we would sin and defy His laws and commands. So, He planned to become human flesh and be the sacrifice for our sin.

The greatest minds in the world, who might have gathered around a conference table to brainstorm an idea to save mankind, would have seemed like fool's play when compared to the ingenious plan of God to redeem us. Man has devised great things, but not as complete and phenomenal as the plan God gave to us, His human creation. Imagine the time that was spent creating the computers we work on and the smartphones we use—all of which are wonderful, but have no saving grace for man's sin problem, and no offer of eternal life. As wonderful as our technology is, it cannot save us. God's plan is so simple that many miss it, yet so powerful, it can save the most wretched person. Indeed, it can save the world! This is love in its truest form.

The resurrection of Jesus after His death is the foundation of the Christian faith. No other religion has documentation of a resurrected savior. The plan of salvation is the greatest blueprint for eternal life the world has ever been offered. It has no bogus edicts or failing survival schemes. We don't need to burn incense or kiss statues, knock on wood, or mutilate our bodies to be saved and have eternal life. Jesus is the way, the truth, and the light. His salvation is not a counterfeit ideology that leaves its followers empty and groping for something more. It's not like the vitamin and mineral concoctions being sold on TV that promise everything but the moon. God's salvation in Jesus is true and dependable, and He gives us the faith to believe. When we trust in Him, His Spirit testifies with our spirit that we are God's children. (Romans 8:16) We know and have strong assurance that we are God's children, and we are saved through that belief.

As perfect as the plan is, God will not be presumptuous and force us to accept it. He gives individuals the freedom of choice—believe or reject. From the beginning, God had the power to create mindless robots that would obey Him simply as He would direct them to obey, but what satisfaction would He have in a world full of robots? What satisfaction would you or I gain by having a robot say to us, "I love you?" Said another way, what pleasure would we have in our personal relationships with other human beings if we mechanically functioned and robotically kissed and hugged each other without any feeling or sensation? God created us in His image, with the same desire for love and companionship that He has. He is no different from us in that He wants our love and our worship. The love and allegiance that God desires are the same as what you and I desire from each other. Not robotic obedience or basic instinct like an animal. What we mortals desire most is for someone to love us unconditionally. God desires the same, and gives us the same. Rest assured in this truth about the unconditional love of God, that He loves the other person in your life as much as He loves you. That's just how He is. It is similar to the love a husband has for his wife or a mother has for her children, but deeper.

In the realm of free will choice, we find the selection of God's design to be the most fascinating characteristic of His human creation. In free choice, we see how much God desires to be loved. Think of it: Before He created mankind, He already had thousands of angels and cherubim and heavenly creatures adoring Him, but none in His image that would have the capacity to love Him in the same detail as He loves us. No living thing would love Him and worship Him like mankind would, whom

He created in His image. As the Bible says, after completing His work in the galaxies and here on earth—including every living thing except human life—He said: "Let us make man in our image and our likeness, and let them rule over the fish of the sea and the birds of the air, over the livestock and over all creatures that move along the ground. So, God created man in his own image, in the image of God he created him; male and female . . ." (Genesis 1:26, 27) God's breath was put into our nostrils and it contains the freedom of choice which makes us unique and separates us from all other species. "Choice" is what brings us to God and "choice" can ultimately separate us from Him.

In the sure reality of a new life in Christ Jesus, all things will become new and changed. God puts a new spirit in the believer's heart and mind. The old sinful habits will fade. There will be new friends because the choices that are made steer in the right direction and the right places, including contact with the right people. God will help smooth out the rough edges. Rejections and persecutions from nonbelievers will come, yet God promises to be all that is needed. He will fill the empty holes and His Holy Word will guide you.

If you have never trusted Jesus Christ as your Savior, why not make that commitment right now? Today is the day of salvation. Tomorrow may be too late. Don't put it off. Simply pray this prayer and receive Christ today:

Lord, I know I am a sinner. I thank You that Jesus died for my sins and took my punishment upon Himself. I ask You to forgive me of my sins and come into my life. I accept Jesus as my Lord and Savior.

If you have prayed this prayer, tell a pastor or a Christian friend and ask for their help and prayers as you begin your new life. Seek out a Bible-believing church.

God bless you.

Discussion

Why is it important to believe in the resurrection of Jesus Christ? Read Matthew 16:18 and share your thoughts about Christ's answer to Peter that "upon this rock I will build my church."

Read Romans 8:16 and write the different ways believers in Jesus are assured they are God's children.

In the realm of free will choice, why do you believe God gave us this freedom?

In what ways does God put a new spirit in the life of a new believer in Him?

About the Author

Mary Cates Haase is a retired Registered Nurse who was born and raised in Detroit, Michigan, yet has lived in many different locations, some as far as Alabama and Florida. Mary, who has one son and two grandsons, recently remarried after the passing of her first husband. Aside from her career as a school nurse, and mother of one son and two grandsons, Mary is a published writer and enjoys an active life in the Presbyterian Church of America. She enjoys the leadership of a weekly bible study group, in various Bible studies. She enjoys her home in southeastern Michigan, in the setting of a beautiful 18-hole golf course.

Visit Mary on her website at
marycateshaaseauthor.com

www.ingramcontent.com/pod-product-compliance
Lightning Source LLC
LaVergne TN
LVHW051704080426
835511LV00017B/2720